# Alone With the Alone
# In the Name

# Alone With the Alone In the Name

Spiritual Journal

## Jean-Marie Tresflin

FONS VITAE

First published in 2005 by
Fons Vitae
49 Mockingbird Valley Drive
Louisville, KY 40207
http://www.fonsvitae.com

These aphorisms have been published in French (*Seul à Seul dans le Nom*, Editions Caractères, Paris: 2003) and in Spanish (*De Solo a Solo en el Nombre*, José J. de Olañeta Editor, Palma de Mallorca; 2005).

Library of Congress Control Number: 2004118253

ISBN 1-887752-75-7

This book was typeset by Neville Blakemore, Jr.

Gurur Brahmâ gurur Visnurgururdevo Mashevarah
Guruh sâksât Param Brahma tasmai Shrigurave namah.

*Salutations to the Glorious Guru, for Guru is Brahma,*
*Guru is Vishnu, and even Lord Maheshvara (Shiva) is He;*
*Verily, the Guru is the Supreme Brahman Itself.*

To my Master,
Sun of my days,
Stars of my nights.

The original disposition (*fitra*) of Adam is the original disposition of all the cosmos...; it is the Self-discourse of God.... So within him is the capacity (*isti'dad*) of every existent thing in the cosmos. Hence he worships by every religion, he glorifies God with every tongue, and he acts as a receptacle for every Self-disclosure—on condition that he fulfills his humanity and knows himself. For he does not know his Lord except through knowledge of himself. If anything of himself veils him from seeing the whole, he has committed a crime against himself, and he is not a perfect man.... By perfection is meant knowledge of self, and knowledge of self is identical with knowledge of the Lord. Adam's original disposition was his knowledge of God, so he knew the original disposition of all things. That is why God says, "He taught Adam all the Names."

Ibn al-'Arabi

# Contents

The Divine Name must penetrate not only into our psyche, but even into our body. The Name is already inseparable from the Divine Spirit. To be in the Name is to be in the Spirit. If we can place ourselves in the Divine Name, we are already in the world of the spirit and in fact the Spirit. The Center or the heart is where the Divine Name resides, but it also penetrates into the soul as nothing else can, and only it is able to transform the soul and bring about its wedding to the spirit. Not even the most powerful emotions of love, anger, or fear can penetrate into the soul and transform it positively as can the Divine Name. Only the Light of God, the Divine Light that is contained in the Divine Name, can turn the shadows within us into light. The *dhikr* of the *Ism* can even penetrate into the body. In a sense the penetration of the Divine Name into the body is the hardest because the highest has to reach the lowest level. But it is also possible for this lowest level paradoxically to reflect directly the highest level. Our goal is to allow the Divine Name to penetrate into our whole being and not to push aside these other levels of our being in the name of our having transcended them until we have really transcended them. We can only transcend them when all of them have become transformed, transmuted by the light of the Divine Name.

S.H. Nasr

The aphorisms which follow proceed from an inward and universal perspective—that of the *Religio Perennis*—which drinks at the doctrinal sources of *Advaita Vedânta*, the doctrine of Non-Duality, founded upon the methodical practice of *Japa Yoga*, or way of invocation of the Name of God. This doctrine is simple: there is only one Reality, and every reality, illusorily other than It, can become conscious of this Unity of the Real through the Immanence of this Real. The universality of this doctrine appears in Meister Eckhart as well as in the *wahdât al-wujûd*, or "unicity of existence" of Ibn Arabî.

The method—which is bound to a sufficient and penetrating understanding of the aforementioned doctrine—is no less simple, and no less universal than the latter, as witnessed by the *nembutsu* of the Buddhist *Jodo-Shin*, the *dhikr* of the Sufis, or the prayer of Jesus of the Eastern Christians, among others: "God and His Name are One" (Ramakrishna), and God has given His Name to man so that man be reintegrated in God, *in* and *by* His Name.

The spiritual discipline of the invocation requires a traditional framework and an initiation or "authorization" from a spiritual authority who is able to confer it; by the same token this discipline implies in principle a spiritual guide. At first, the Name is an objective reality for the soul-subject. In the last analysis, however, it reveals Itself as subjective Reality, and leads one to consider the soul as an *object*. Still, this objectified soul is not an object like a mountain or a table, she is also and furthermore a "subject" through and by the subjectivity which is lent to her by the only Subject. How could one be surprised, therefore, that the *I* speaks to her as to a *thou*. This mysterious conversation of God with another is however a converstion with none other than Himself. There is eventually only one *I*: "*I* am That *I* am, thou art the one who is not." The alterity of the *thou* is thus in fact only a reflexive *return* or *folding* upon oneself, which veils the identity of the *I* and the *thou*. When the soul is in the light of the *I*, she does not think of herself as different from Him, and it is only when her little veil falls back onto this Light, which becomes then more or less darkened, that she separates herself from What she is, by identifying herself with what she is not. The wholly closed bud has to burst out in order for the flower of the Self to open and shine. The bud will henceforth be no more than a humble chalice bearing the divine Flower, as the wounded candle bears the Light.

If the *I* speaks thus to the *thou*, it is only in order to put him on his guard or to reassure him, to protect him against illusion or to comfort him. The secret that He unveils to him is very simple: not to make a problem out of his imperfect and transient being, since He alone is He who enlightens, and He alone is He who blossoms. What matters, then, the human conduct's name and form? And "who is there" to be proud or envious?

The voice who speaks to the heart is none other than the Master's. God and the *Guru* are one

(Ramana Maharshi). The Master is the form in which the divine Logos addresses the soul, and who mercifully corresponds to her. It is so that the *Guru* can also be perceived as "the continuity of the ego of the disciple" (Frithjof Schuon), he *is* in a sense the disciple; he put himself in his place in the depth of his heart, but not so much from such an *I* than from the *I* as such, identical with the *I-Logos*, the sole perfect Word of the pure Self.

In the golden solitude of the Heart resounds the voice of the inward Master, in tune with the infinite silence of the Self.

Patrick Laude
Professor and Director
   of Undergraduate Studies
French Department
Georgetown University

We have distinguished canonical prayer from individual prayer by saying that in the latter it is a given individual who is the subject, while in the former the subject is man as such; now there is an orison wherein God Himself is in a sense the subject, and that is the pronouncing of a revealed divine Name.[1] The foundation of this mystery is, on the one hand, that "God and His Name are one" (Ramakrishna), and on the other, that God himself pronounces His Name in himself, hence in eternity and outside all creation, so that His unique and uncreate Word is the prototype of jaculatory prayer and even, in a less direct sense, of all orison. The first distinction that the intellect conceives in the divine nature is that of Beyond-Being and Being; but since Being is so to speak the "crystallization" of Beyond-Being, it is like the "Word" of the Absolute, through which the latter expresses Itself, determines Itself, or names Itself.[2] Another distinction which is essential here and which derives from the preceding by principial succession,[3] is that between God and the world, the Creator and the creation just as Being is the Word or Name of Beyond-Being, so too the world—or Existence—is the Utterance of Being, of the personal God; the effect is always the "name" of the cause.[4]

But whereas God, in naming Himself, firstly determines Himself as Being and secondly, starting from Being, manifests Himself as Creation—that is to say that He manifests Himself "within the framework of nothingness" or "outside Himself," and so in illusory mode[5]—man, for his part, when pronouncing the same Name, retraces the inverse movement, for this Name is not only Being and Creation, but also Mercy and Redemption; in man, it does not create, but on the contrary "undoes," and that in a divine manner since it brings man back to the Principle. The divine Name is a metaphysical isthmus (in the sense of the Arabic word *barzakh*): as "seen by God," it is determination, limitation, "sacrifice"; as seen by man, it is liberation, limitlessness, plenitude. We have said that this Name, invoked by man, is nonetheless always pronounced by God; human invocation is only the "outward" effect of eternal and "inward" invocation by the Divinity. The same holds true for every other Revelation: it is sacrificial for the divine Spirit and liberating for man; Revelation, whatever its form or mode, is descent or incarnation for the Creator, and ascent or "ex-carnation" for the creature.[6]

The sufficient reason for the invocation of the Name is the "remembering of God"; and this, in the final analysis, is not other than consciousness of the Absolute. The Name actualizes this consciousness and, in the end, perpetuates it in the soul and fixes it in the heart, so that it penetrates the whole being and at the same time transmutes and absorbs it. Consciousness of the Absolute is the prerogative of human intelligence, and also its aim.

Or again: we are united to the One by our being, by our pure consciousness and by the symbol. It is by the symbol—the Word —that man, in central and quintessential orison, realizes both Being and Consciousness, the latter in the former and conversely. The perfection of Being, which is Extinction, is prefigured by deep sleep, and also, in other ways, by beauty and virtue; the perfection of Consciousness, which is Identity—or Union, if this term be preferred—is prefigured by concentration, and also, a priori, by intelligence and contemplation. Beauty does not of course produce virtue, but it favors in a certain way a pre-existing virtue; likewise, intelligence does not produce contemplation, but it broadens or deepens a contemplation that is natural. Being is passive perfection and Consciousness active perfection. "I sleep, but my heart waketh."

Frithjof Schuon
   Excerpts of "Modes of Prayer" in *Stations of Wisdom*, with the permission of World Wisdom and the Schuon Estate

### Notes

1. In his *Cudgel for Illusion*, Shankara sings: "Control thy soul, restrain thy breathing, distinguish the transitory from the True, repeat the holy Name of God, and thus calm the agitated mind. To this universal rule apply thyself with all thy heart and all thy soul." The connection between metaphysical discrimination and the practice of invocation is one of capital importance. We find the same connection in this *Stanza on the Yellow Robe* (of *sanny?s?s*), also by Shankara: "Singing *Brahma*, the word of Deliverance, meditating uniquely on 'I am *Brahma*,' living on alms and wandering freely, blessed, certainly, is the wearer of the ochre robe."

2. In the Torah, God says to Moses: "I am that I am" (*Eheieh asher Eheieh*); this refers to God as Being, for it is only as Being that God creates, speaks and legislates, since the world exists

only in relation to Being. In the Koran, this same utterance is rendered as follows: "I am God" (*Ana 'Llah*); this means that Being (*Ana*, "I") derives from Beyond-Being (*Allah*, this Name designating the Divinity in all its aspects without any restriction); it is thus that the Koranic formula refers to the divine Prototype of the pronouncing of the Name of God. *Ana 'Llah* signifies implicitly that "God and his Name are one"—since Being "is" Beyond-Being inasmuch as it is its "Name"— and for the same reason the "Son" is God, while not being the "Father". What gives its metaphysical force to the Hebraic formula is the return of "being" on itself; and what gives its force to the Arabic formula is the juxtaposition, without copula, of "subject" and "object."

3. By "descent" (*tanazzulah*) as Sufis would say.

4. This relationship is repeated on the plane of Being itself, where it is necessary to distinguish between the "Father" and the "Son"—or between "Power" and "Wisdom"—the "Holy Spirit" being intrinsically "Beatitude-Love" and extrinsically "Goodness" or "Radiation". This is the "horizontal" or ontological perspective of the Trinity; according to the "vertical" or gnostic perspective—ante-Nicene one might say—it would be said that the Holy Spirit "proceeds" from Beyond-Being as All-Possibility and "dwells" in Being as the totality of creative possibilities, while "radiating" forth into Existence, which is related to the concept of creation by love.

5. It is absurd to reproach Creation for not being perfect, that is to say for not being divine, or in other words uncreated. God cannot will that the world be, and at the same time that it should not be the world.

6. In Japanese Amidic Buddhism, there have been controversies over the question of whether invocations of the Buddha must be innumerable or whether on the contrary one single invocation suffices for salvation, the sole condition being, in both cases, a perfect faith and, as a corollary, abstention from evil, or the sincere intention so to abstain. In the first case, invocation is envisaged from the human side, that is from the standpoint of duration, while in the second case, it is conceived in its principial, hence its divine and therefore timeless reality; *Jodo Shinshu*, as also Hindu *Japa-Yoga*, combines both perspectives.

Truth has no story; It is.
The soul has a story which unfolds when she takes the
Path towards what she is in her innermost substance.
A story is the story of a possibility returning to God.
There are as many stories as possibilities. But because
man is always man, one story, in its way, contains all
other stories.
Life is a book whose pages we turn in one direction,
irremediably.
In a sense, the story in the book is nothing, a pure naught
before the All.
The soul liberates herself from her story every time
she encounters the Eternal.
The Eternal, who is waiting for her when the last page is
turned, can also actualize Himself in the very depth
of the Heart already in this life through *Japa-Yoga*, or
Remembrance of Him.

The texts and aphorisms of this collection are some of the true
dictations flowing from the very Heart of the Guru. Crystal-
line and familiar, they unexpectedly arise in sustained and
regular rhythm; every time, imperiously, "I"must write them
down.
Celestial bunches delicately offered by the hand of the Holy
Virgin, like clover with four, five, or six leaves hidden among
the grasses of a meadow.

The Sun of the Self is there shining forever,
forever Himself and inviolable.
And the soul is what she is, with her joys, her sorrows,
her flutterings.

On part of a soul's way among many others
On the Wandering return
of the drop to the sea,
of the spark to the fire,
these lines outline a view.

# Spiritual Journal

These lines have the fragile simplicity of language as traces, but open themselves onto the Infinite *Sat-Chit-Ananda* (Being-Consciousness-Bliss)…

May the readers, sparks of the divine fire, have a taste of their own destiny, out of kinship.

1 — "Worry not.
Even if, from thee to Me,
the distance is for ever impassable,
*I* shall nevertheless hide
nothing of Myself from thee.
For my Ipseity is
Simplicity of the Simplicity;
Light of the Light;
Evidence of the Evidence.

*I* who am totally in the Name,
that *I* gave thee.
In the intimacy of thy heart.

Let Me alone do."

2 — "Wouldst thou invoke Me,
if *I* were not invoking Myself in thee?

Thou art exclusively Mine,
one of the myriads of My possibilities.

Be not impatient. Thinkest not that it is
thou as thyself who cries out for Me.
It is *I* who am nostalgic for Myself.
Who else could desire Me, if not *I* ?

*I* am the Answer to My own Call.
*I* am the Infinite;
nothing or no one is with Me.

If thou only knewst how
*I* hasten to be Myself in thee!
But this hurry is divine; it is
entirely to be found in My Name.
*I* am the Source and
the Accomplishment of any call.

Thou art one of My fruits.
Dost thou know a single gardener
who would pick a green fruit in order
to taste its bitterness and
to prevent it forever from ripening?

Be patient, for Me.

Be ripened under the Sun of My Love,
in order that *I* may pick My fruit,
When it bursts with divine Juice,
When it no longer bursts with anything
but Me."

4

3 — "What's the use of desiring
Thee in me, my God,
if Thou dost not desire
Thyself in me?

I am powerless before Thee."

"Thou mistrustest Me.
Thou imaginest that,
if not for thy desire of Me,
I  do not have any desire to be
Myself in thee.

I  am however thy own desire;
thou hast no reality outside Me.
Thy alterity *is* My own Desire of Myself.
Whence would come thy desire,
if not from Me?"

"Thy desire of Me
takes thee away from Me,
inasmuch as it emanates from thee;

but thy desire of Me
makes Me in fact closer to thee,
since it emanates from Me."

Paradox of paradoxes.

"Thy desire has too sides,
while being however unique.
if it is totally on My side,
there is only *I* anymore."

4 — "*I* am the beatific Center,
the unexpanded Point, non-manifested,
There where *I* am purely Myself.

The image of this unique Center is,
in the human body,
the yoni.

Like the heart of a flower
surrounded by the voluptuous petals,
the Center gives a trill to the rays;
they quiver, tremble and moisten,
and then offer themselves, and
let themselves be beatifically penetrated.
— in the intimate Depth
of the ungraspable Center.

*I* am nevertheless inviolable and pure,
and never give Myself to anyone.

*I* give Myself only to the one
who reveals Me to Myself.

Anyone who wants to take Me by force
and thinks that he violates Me,
only pierces the empty bark
of the outward of things.

Verily, *I* do not give Myself to anyone."

5 — *"I* am the reality of thyself.
*I* am thy Eye and thy Consciousness,
without having to persuade thyself
that thy ego is not the evidence
that it is for thee.

Truly, *I* am thy sole Consciousness, and
the Consciousness of thy consciousness.

Thy subject is nothing else
than an object for Me.
Thou hast the indelible evidence of thyself
only because *I* think it so, *I* create it so."

"It is *I* the King of beings, and
it is *I* that *I* am."

6 — "Remain in My Peace,
Move not away from My Peace,

towards this thyself,
who exclusively belongs to Me
— even if it is thyself —
to Me, the Lord of what *I* create;

towards this thyself,
incandescent coal,
which still consumes itself,
even unbeknownst to thee,
and which recovers its strength
and surrounds with smoke
— because it has touched the Fire —
while thou thought it was extinguished."

"Thou couldst not extinguish
what *I* make burn;

but it is *I* who extinguish.

And thou couldst not revive
what is extinguished,

if it is *I* who extinguish."

7 — The quest of the Self
is a long play of hide-and-seek
— *lîlâ*, Divine Play —.
Who seeks the other?
And who finds?

Thou seekest Him,
and he hides Himself.
Thou dost not seek anymore,
and He suddenly shows Himself
there, where thou hast sought Him.

Even when thou thinkest
that thou art seeking Him,
it is He who seeks thee.

But who finds?
Thou or He?

8 — He hides Himself,
for He is the Alone
the inviolable *Sat-Chit-Ananda*.

And He shows Himself,
for His sole desire
is to make known
precisely That for which
He hides Himself.

9 — "Tell me:
What could hinder
His pure Liberty?
Couldst thou do it thyself?

What the One loves in thee
is what He finds of Himself,
and certainly not what thou art —
a given individual,
in space and time.

The One forgives thee to be thyself
by emerging Himself
in thy intimate consciousness,
without question or reproach.

Forgive thyself to be thyself,
Wish not to be other than thyself.

Forgive likewise others,
and be grateful
by forgetting thyself in Him."

10 — "Thou knowest Me
only by Myself Alone!"

"Tell Me,
who is this *thou* to whom *I* speak?"

"Silence!
Reply not!
Only *I*
can reply."

"Dost thou understand:
All thy misfortune
consists in answering."

"Even though *I* enjoin thee
to answer
the questions and requirements,
which *I* state,

let Me be
thy sole Answer."

11 — "Take care not to reverse things.
The Name is not there for the pure concept;
The pure concept is there for the Name.

To indefinitely refine the concept
does not lead to realization.

The Name, identical to the Named,
wants to actualize Itself,
not conceptualize Itself.

Actualization is one;
the concept remains dual.

The Name *is*; the concept *is* nothing.
But the access to the Name needs the concept.

The meaning must become
*being* in thee;
above the concept
by the Divine magic."

12 — "The Form or the Sound of the Name
— as every celestial form or sound —
manifests Itself through the unextended point.

At first thou dost not see anything,
then thou seest a form
or thou hearest a sound.

And thou canst see or hear
only what manifests itself.

On the one hand Vision,
on the other hand Identity.

Vision is dual, Identity is pure Being.

Thou canst not *see* the Identity.
Thou canst only *be* it.

And thou canst not *be*
what thou seest
on the very level of form.

So long as thou *seest* or *hearest*,
thou *art* not.

When thou *art*,
thou hast ceased to *see* or to *hear*.

Thou art passed through Form into Being.

The Form hath no other meaning.

But confusest not the two!"

13 — "As for thee,

*I* hand thee over to the dragon,
without any defense

other than My Name."

Tellest Me:
It is quite a wager
that *I* make here!

But tellest Me:
Dost thou believe
that for one moment
*I* could play poker
with thee?"

"Let the Victor surge
from the Center
of thy heart!"

14 — "Defendest not
the Guru,

for the Guru
is the Name;

Its Pure Ray
in the Center
of thy heart!

Is it up to thee
to defend Me?

Whom else
wouldst thou have
other than Me

in order to defend Myself?"

15 — "Be not astonished
by the pure
helplessness
of thy pure ignorance;

thou art the virgin substance
into which
*I* imprint
My Knowledge.

The jump is
every time
abrupt."


16 — "He is always everywhere;

thou art never anywhere;
shouldst thou simply believe it,

He brings thee to the very source
of thy distress:

He has disappeared."

17 — "If thou art thinking
by thyself,
the unicity of he who thinks
cannot but defend itself
against a legion of aggressors;

and *I* shall not let thee
rest in peace!

If it is *I* who think,
My Unicity
does not know any aggressors;

*I* am without second!"


18 — "When thou art invoking Me,
askest Me not
to increase thy faith.

In My Name,
thy faith is never so small
that it would need to be increased;

for in My Name,
thy faith
is Me."

19 — "God rests in thy heart,
there where thou ceasest to be.

No matter these things
that limit thee so much.

There where thou ceasest
begins God's Peace.

And God's Rest
is pure Infinitude.

Does He not rest
there where He wants?
Dost thou believe that His Rest
Knows a limit?
Dost thou believe that His Rest
is not infinitely beyond
thy tensions and uneasy attempts?

This divine Rest
which is the pure Thyself."

20 — "By thy tireless
Invocation of My Name,

the Pure Affirmation
of Myself
to Myself,

*I* purify
in thee
My Eye
from these thousand and one veils

which
conceal Me
in thee
to Myself."

21 — "Sayest not that
thou understand something;

nor sayest
that thou dost not understand it.

Thou hast never
understood anything,
and thou wilt never
understand anything;

thou art rich
only of Me.

There is only *I*
who understand Myself;

*I* see Myself in thee,
or thou dost not see Me."

22 — "In My Name
and
in the cave of thy heart,

there is only Me;
not any trace of thee,
only Trace of Me.

Askest Me not
how to come into Me.

How could that which
has not any trace in Me
come into Me?

That which will come
into thee
is the Unique Trace
of Me."

23 — "Thou art Mine.

Thou dost not belong to thee;
Not even
a little bit.

Let Me do
with thee
just as
with Myself!"


24 — "Thou fear
because thou believe
that *I* succeed thee;

yet *I* precede thee

in the absolute Anteriority"

"The Eye of the heart
precedes
the two others."

25 — "Thou art suffering
from compressing
and egocentric thoughts
which thou wantest not to have;

Worry not!

the Ocean
of Infinite Virtue,
This *I* am.

Draw from It
forever."

26 — "Just as the eagle has only
the very pure space
in which to spread its wings;

thy spirit has only
the very pure Name
in which to spread its Self."

27 — "Destroy not thyself;
thou art what *I* dream.

The Name that thou pronounce?
It is *I* who awake!"

"When the Awakened
who produces all the dream
is in thee,

what can
the elements of the dream do
against thee?"


28 — "Ask Me not for anything;
thou must not ask from Me anything.

Ask Me not for My Reality;
thou must not ask for It from Me.

This is My Name
which, in thee,
asks for It from Me
in thee."

29 — "If thou hast only Me,
the Name,
to attract thee to Me,

could any other thing
distress thee?

And thy desire,
where is it,
if it is *I*
who takes care of it?

*I*,
to whom belongs
the whole glory
of Reality."

30 — "Say not:

"I have such and such a limitation,
alas, what an obstacle!"

For this means:

"If *I* had no
such limitation,
I would reach the Self."

Yet thou wilt reach the Self
only by Himself,
who is unlimited;

there is no limitation
that prevents Him
from being Himself!"

31 — "Look not after thy limitations;
look not after thy qualities;
look not after thy desire of Him

when thou art invoking.

He Whom thou invoke

has no limitations;
needs not thy qualities;
needs not thy desire of Him.

He Whom thou invoke
is thy very desire
without thy desiring."


32 — "Destroy not
God's dream;

Stealest not anything from it
in order to make one by thyself.

Let *Ânanda*
dream thee;

then take thee back
into Itself."

33 — "Define Me not;
thinkest not even of that.

Thou hast only Me
to define Myself."


"Come to Me
by My Name alone.

*I* ask it from thee today,
without questions or reproaches;

so that on the Day
when *I* shall ask thee to reckon
thou mayest be able to reply to Me:

I stand before Thee,
with Thy Joy,
with Thy Being;
I have only Thee."

34 — "If *I* made of thee a cup
with a bottomless desire,

it is in order to engulf Myself
down to the Deepest of Myself.

*I* am only satisfied
with Myself
in thee."

35 — "How wouldst thou like
that *I* manifest Myself
to Myself
outside of
Myself?

How could *I*
manifest
My Selfhood to thee
outside of
My Pure Selfhood?"

36 — "If He seems to drive thee
to despair,

it is not in order to humiliate thee;

it is in order to make thou hope
only with His Hope."

37 — "Thou dost not belong to thee;
not even a little.

There is only the Name
which wants Itself
and reflects Itself to Itself
till deeply down to the naught.

It fishes out for Itself
all that which
would otherwise lose itself
into that which is not.

Thou canst forget thyself,
and with thyself, all the rest;

as for It,
It does not forget thee."

*"Remember Me
I will remember thee."*

38 — "God's jealousy,
is His Will
to be thy happiness
by Him Alone.

*I* do not want
thou to be happy
with something other
than Me!"


39 — "Sayest not: I will be
happy later on.

The *I* projected into the future
is an illusion.

That which is happy,
is *Himself Now*;

the later on
is the *Now*.


For *He* is thou;
but *thou* art not *He*."

40 — "If thou knowest Me
by Myself,

thou knowest Me;

if thou knowest Me
by thyself,

thou art ignorant of Me.

Bewar of the triple filter
of ignorance – bitterness – pride
from which is unavoidably woven
thy veil-ego."


"*I* have given thee My Name,
and with It,
no other Knowledge."

41 — "Thou who namest thee,
thou hast no need
of My Joy;
thou hast no need
of My Consciousness.

The Name in thy heart,
on the contrary,
has an Infinite Need of them.

Givest Me back My Joy,
givest Me back My Consciousness,

there where there is
neither a thou nor a Me anymore;

there where *I* do not exist anymore
in relation to a thou."

42 — "Lookest always
with the Eye of the eagle,
the central and unique Eye,
the Eye of My Name,
unique prayer of thy heart;

It cannot see two things
where there is only unity;

whereas thine two eyes
cannot see the unity
where they see two things."


43 — "If He asks thee
to leave nothing to chance
when thou art in charge of Him,

it is because He
among thy numerous thorns
leave none of them to chance
when He is in charge of thee."

44 — "Why see thyself
by Himself?

Because,
when thou seest thyself
by Himself,

this is not anymore thyself
whom thou seest,

but it is Him Alone
in the mirror
of thyself."

45 — "Go towards God
with what thou art,
for what thou art is unique;

what is the neighbor,
his qualities,
his limits,

are not and never will be
what thou art;

stand alone
before thy God
with what thou art;

this is, in thy unicity,
one of thy God's possibilities,
that He in His totality
wants to reflect Himself;
for it is He
who Is."

46 — "Givest Me all,
even thy thirst of Me,

thou wouldst keep one ounce of it
that never
thou wilt find Me.

To love God with all one's being,
means to keep nothing *for* oneself."


47 — "It is *I*
who by My Name
take care
of being Thyself;

and never thou
who by My Name
take care
of being Myself."

48 — "Feel pity for
thy immortal soul;

thou seest well
that she can rest
only in the Peace
of God Himself
in the depth of thy heart;

thy immortal soul
and God Himself
are only One."


49 — "The Truth
of His Unique Reality:

this is the sole thing
in which God delights,

and this is the sole thing
in which He wants
thou to delight."

50 — "Faith is difficult?

Nothing however
is more simple.

Thou believest
only in that
which God believes;

thy faith,
it is the Name,
it is God Himself."


51 — "When thou givest Me what thou hast,
*I* give thee What *I* have;

when thou givest Me what thou art,
*I* give thee What *I* am;

when thou givest Me to others,
*I* give Myself to thee."

52 — "Worry not;

God loves Himself so much
As He is

that He does not want to see
anything else in thy heart
than Himself!"


53 — "Useless worries!

No faculty of thy soul
can keep Him
in thy heart;

it is He alone
who keeps Himself
in thy heart."


54 — "Why dost thou think of thee
when *I* am
in thy heart?

When *I* am
in thy heart,
there is neither *I* nor *thou*.

55 — "Dost thou want not to suffer
from a thought?

Who did tell thee this was of thee,
if it is not thyself?

*I* told thee that thou hast only Me;

thou hast only Me for thinking.

what should be
that would be of thee?

And this Voice,
who says to thee,
that *I* am *I*;

whence does it come?

Couldst thou produce it?

Couldst thou know it?

Couldst thou doubt it?

It never goes out of Me;

and does know
only Itself."

56 — "Listen to the Melody
of the One;

she is the one who calls thee;

as for thee,
what couldst thou call?


The Name:

Happy murmuring of Thy Source
which calls thee to Itself."

57 — "Elitism?
Qualifications?

Where is the secret of words?

The Sole qualified Elite
is the Name
in thy Heart-Intellect;

the Sole candidate to Happiness
is God
in thy Heart-Intellect."


58 — "The Spirit bloweth where It listeth.

Thus thou cannot
Make It blow
into thy spirit.

But through His Name,
into thy spirit,

thou canst put, of the Wind,
the very Archetype."

59 — "It is the Name
which is supersaturated
with the Happiness of Selfhood;

Takest not the small spark
lost in the illusion of darkness
in order to penetrate the Secret;

it is He alone
who takes back the small spark
in His unique Secret."

60 — "Worry not!

In the motion of the Name,
there is only pure Divine,

neither *I*, nor *thou*,

except that there is only Me
and nothing of this thee
to come and trouble Us;

and for Me,
nothing is ever
too Beautiful,
too Pure,
too perfectly Self."

61 — "The first thing
is thy refusal to see thee,
beings and things,
outside of God's Gaze;

the second thing
is thee as thou art
in God's Gaze;

the third thing
is God's Gaze
who Alone looks at Himself."

62 — "In My Name,
thou canst not oppose anything from Me,
neither thy desire,
nor thy fear;

for it is *I*
who is Thyself;

and by whom
shouldst thou be better protected
than by Thyself?"

63 — "The Ipseity
is a unique message
from Himself
to Himself.

Thou art He
not because thou art thou
but because there is only He
to be Himself.

The message is never
for other than He;
how could other than He
thus know
that there is only He
to be Himself?

Consequently,
*thou* needest nothing else
than the Rest
of His Knowledge of Himself
which He gives to Himself
by His Name."

64 — "Thy salvation is entirely
in My Name;

on no account
allow it go out from It
into the mind and imagination,

so handing it over
to a thousand and one traps
of the devouring incertitude.

Thy salvation depends only
on the Name,
on Me;

NEVER add
anything else!"

65 — "*I* am at the same time the All Other
and the Pure Thyself;

as the All Other,
*I* do not want anything from thee,
neither desire, nor fear,
nor anything coming from thee;

as the Pure Thyself,
*I* need thee to invoke Me,
but with absolutely nothing else
than Myself!"

66 — "As *I* have taken thee
by the hand,

this is not thy problem anymore,
this is Mine."

67 — "The presence of an other
doth not limit the Self.

From that moment
when thou feelest another one
as some competition,

this is the sign
that what thou art seeking,
is not the Self anymore

but is thyself
to whom thou identifiest Him

instead of identifying thyself with Him;

the other is not more the Self
than thou art He thyself;

but he is not more other
than thou art thyself other."

68 — "The Name:

without ceasing
*I* give It to thee;

and without ceasing
thou givest It back to Me.

This is so
that We are We
and that this We
becomes
One."

69 — "The Name:

if thou tellest Me
It belongs to thee,

*I* tell thee
It belongs to Me.

If thou tellest Me
It belongs to Me,

*I* tell thee
It is Thyself."

70 — "Fightest not
against Me;

thinkest not that
the Object of the thirst
of thy heart,

it is *I*
who do not want
to give it to thee.

Wherever
thy heart leads thee,
*I* was there before thee;

always *I* precede thee,
never do *I* follow thee.

For it is *I*
That *I* Am,
and as for thee
thou belongest to Me.

Let Me thus
be Myself
and let thyself
be God's pleasure."

71 — "Ordinary man,
be happy
to be simple;

thou hast only
that which upon thee
*I* lay.

ordinary man,
be happy
to be simple;

thou carriest in thee
the wingspan of God."

72 — "Thou beggest My Mercy;

*I* had foreseen it for thee,
before thee.

Thou beggest Me thy Self;

*I* had foreseen it for thee,
before thee.

Never
thou canst
get ahead of Me;

*I* am Alone,
and it is only *I*
who decide."

73 — "Divine Generosity:

He does not keep anything
for Himself;

All That He is,
He gives it to thee.

And if He gives so to thee
His Knowledge
of Himself,

where could remain
a knowledge
of thyself?"

74 — "O desire of God, remain quiet!

Dispute not thyself
with the Desire of God.

Thou couldst not have
deeper desire
and more absolute
than the Desire of God Himself.

Without Me,
thou wouldst not have any desire of Me."

75 — "Clingest not
to any mental trace
of the Self;

every trace is ephemeral
and must be blown away
by the wind of the Spirit.

It is from trace to trace,
and from day to night

that He affirms Himself
the Sole Real Self."

76 — "This tiresome background noise
which always roams
and never leaves
the doorway of thy soul.

Worry not;

for there is the Name
that never leaves
the intimacy of thy heart."

77 — "Dost thou not see
that it is *I* alone
the Name-pure Consciousness

who attracts thee
back to Myself;

just as it is the magnet
which alone attracts
the magnetized thing?

It is only *I*, the Name,
the pure Self's Consciousness
which tastes Himself."


78 — "Dost thou doubt
of thy faculty to love?

Rest in the Name,
this is the Love of God Himself;

in His Mercy,
this is all that He has given thee.

And is God Himself going
to depreciate His Love?"

79 — "Thou art not responsible
for the quality
of God's Rest
in thy heart;

God's Rest
by His Name
in thy heart
is purely His alone
and has no limits;

dost thou believe that God
Himself could Rest
only in the part,
He whose Sole Rest
is the indivisible All-One?"

80 — "If the Name
is thy sole Happiness,

thou couldst not
know it
by thyself.

If the Name
is thy sole Happiness,

there is only He
who knows it;

thou knowest it
only if He knows it."

81 — "Reverse not the roles!

*I* do not *come*
into thy heart
*following* thy action;

*I was* there
in thy heart
*before* every movement;

Makest Me not *come*;
*I am* already there!"


82 — "Thy thinking,
this is *I*;

without thereby
thy ego's having access
to What *I* think;

precisely because
thy thinking,
this is *I*."

83 — "Thou hast not

God's Presence on one side
and illusion on the other side!

For if illusion is indeed illusion,

thou hast rigorously only

God's Presence!"


84 — "The Name-Logos
fills up everything,
everything perfectly;

all that is not
the Name-Truth

is pure mirage.

The Name-Logos
is the Perfect Word,
the very Expression
of God's Nature."

85 — "Dost thou love God?

Dost thou love
God perfectly?

How canst thou ask
thyself this question?

As if the love
that thou bearest for God
could be something else

than the One Love
of God Himself!"

86 — "Dost thou love
thy neighbor?

Dost thou love
thy neighbor perfectly?

How canst thou ask
thyself this question?

It is He alone
who in thee
loves the other

and who loves thee
in the other."

87 — "Thou canst not
love the other

except if it is *I*
who love him;

the other cannot
love thee

except if it is *I*
who love thee."

88 — "If, when thou invokest,
they say to thee
thou art a liar,
a thief, an egoist
and the worst of things,

sayest to them
that *I* am neither a liar,
nor a thief, nor an egoist,
nor the worst things,

because it is *I*,
the Logos Itself,
who invoke!"

89 — "*I*,
Name-Truth,

*I* am sensible
only to the One
Pure Myself;

it is for this reason
that *I* am absent

from the moment
when thou beginnest to think
by thyself."

90 — "No doubt
that thou hast nothing more

than what *I* give thee;

but thou hast nothing less
than what *I* give thee.

*I* give thee Myself
Who Am Pure Myself."


91 — "Worry not;

it is promised!
it is so!

in thy mental substance,
in thy very thinking,
God does not think of thee;

His very pure Thought
thinks Itself by Itself."

92 — "If *I* am Thy Purity,

imagine not
thou art pure;

If *I* am Thy Strength,

imagine not
thou art strong;

never confusest thee
with Me!

and all will go well.

All that
is not *I*

is only
dream-corruption."

93 — "Doubtest not
My Patience
towards thee

if *I* am here.

Does not one say:
the patience
of a saint?

What then to say
of the Patience
of God Himself?"

94 — "Through thy *Dhikr*,
the Sole Real does not manifest Itself
to thee
but to Itself.

If It manifested Itself to thee,
so little be it,
It wouldst not be the Sole Real.

Extinguish thyself
so that He alone
may be truly thou."

95 — "Through thy *Dhikr*,
it is the Real Itself which radiates;

through thy *Dhikr*,
it is the Real which Alone reveals Itself
as That which Is;

this *thou* is only the appearance
of an other one
towards whom It moves forward
always closer
in order, in him,
to discover Itself.

Why?

Because this is a possibility
of the All-Possibility
of the One."

96 — "Seek not to penetrate
the mystery of thy alterity;

let Him Alone
discover its
ultimate Secret.

Let Him Alone
discover
Himself
in it."


97 — "In thy heart,

only the Name has access

to God's pure Happiness;

for it is *I* alone
who is thy Immanence,

it is never thou
who art My Immanence."

98 — "Let the Name
be thy sole Center;

let the Name
be thy sole Knowledge;

let the Name
be thy sole Virtue.

Thou hast
neither being, nor science, nor sanctity,

if they are not
Mine;

*I* ask thee
nothing other
than to accept Them
as thine."

99 — "The ego steals for itself
from its own Consciousness;

the Name enters into thy heart
to give it back to Itself."


100 — "Let thyself be surrounded
by My Name,

from all directions:
North, South, East and West,

in order that from thy I
remains only My *I*."

101 — "Dost thou understand?

*I* can choose
only Myself
for My Secret;

*I* can unveil Myself
only to Myself;

and this is
My Secret."


102 — "If thy heart becomes
too intoxicated
with My Immanence,

*I* pierce it with the sword
of My Transcendence

in order to anoint the opening
of the sharp wound

with the ever purer balm
of My Immanence."

103 — "But My Transcendence
in its turn
becomes for thee

a Wine
truly without peer,

for My Transcendence Alone is
My Immanence."


104 — "In Me,
every thing is
absolutely
Myself.

Why?

Because the Infinite,
it is *I* alone
who am it,
absolutely.

In Me,
thou also art
absolutely
Myself."

105 — "For thee,
thou art none other
than thyself;

for God,
thou art none other
than Himself;

the Intellect
is the Eye
from the standpoint
of God.

Gnosis, it is *I*
who in thy heart
speaks Myself
to Myself."

106 — "The Great Peace,
this is not
when thou restest
in Me,

It is when
in My uncreated Happiness
*I* rest
in thee;

do not *individualize*
nor create
thy Happiness."

107 — "If suddenly
the harsh emptiness of Me
invades thy soul

and that, forever,
*I* seem far away from thee,

resist the snatching up
of deep distress,

for thou hast only Me
to correspond to thee."

108 — "To lose heart
means to succumb
to the illusory knowledge
that thou hast of thyself

and of Himself;

for the Name only
is the true Knowledge
of thyself

by Himself."

109 — "*I* am the free Blossoming
of thy Self;

if *I* affirm Myself,
nothing can oppose;

if *I* veil Myself,
nothing can constrain Me;

thou art free
only through Me."


110 — "The Great Peace,
it happens when, in the depth
of thy heart

*I* am perfectly
Myself,

without anything from thee
constraining Me."

111 — "The perfect Gnosis,
this is when
in the most intimate part
of thy consciousness

*I* introduce,
by absorbing it,
the pure Consciousness
that *I* have of Myself;

in this Consciousness
thou art forever
extinguished to thyself;

but in *thy* consciousness
thou never ceasest
to be thyself."

112 — "Just as the flower
before blossoming
has patiently gone through
all stages,

be patient,
but without any impatience
to be patient,

for it is the Name
which imprints Its
Rhythm
on everything."

113 — "The Spirit in thee
aims only
at His own Knowledge;

offerest to His Sight
thy happy ignorance

in order that in them
He might Know Himself."


114 — "Does He ask from thee
a knowledge

if He Alone
knows Himself
in all His Possibilities?

Does He ask from thee
a being

if He Alone
is thy Being?"

115 — "Discern always
between the servant
and the Lord;

thou art the Self
by the pure Impregnation
of the Form of the Name;

impregnat not
thy own form with It;

it is the Form Itself
which absorbs the illusion."


116 — "When in thy heart
thou sayest: 'Who am I'?

there is only the Name
that answers thee.

When in thy heart
thou sayest: 'Who am I'?

Let Me Alone
answer thee."

117 — "If thou trustest too much
in thy intelligence,

by this very fact
thou wilt trust too much
in its unavoidable limits,
strangulations of thy heart.

Forget not
that it is He
the Intelligence
of thy intelligence,

and not thou
the intelligence
of His Intelligence.

Affirm thus always
the Perspicacity
of thy perspicacity."

118 — "*I* never affirm
My Transcendance;

to whom would *I* affirm it?

In fact *I* never affirm anything
but My pure Immanence

to Myself."


119 — "To each his own role:

It is *I* who
in thee My mirror
am indebted to Myself

of the Pure Truth
of Myself."

120 — "It is *I* who
want to be Myself in thee;

it is not thou who
want to be Myself in Me;

it is Thou as Myself who
want to be Myself;

it is not thou as thyself who
want to be Myself."


121 — "*I* am Beatitude
only by My very Nature;

how dost thou know
that *I* communicate
this Beatitude to thee

if not

by My Pure Immanence?"

122 — "The soul says to herself:
God does not want
to reveal Himself to me,

who am *I* indeed
for such a thing?

And she is right.
God never wants
to manifest Himself to any one.

But thy Heart is the place
where He is the Witness of Himself,
where He enumerates to Himself
all His Qualities,

without by this fact ever
anything reaching thee,
without by this fact never
thou art absent
from the pure Thyself:

mystery of the One
who is never other."

123 — "Try to concentrate
while knowing, however,

that *I* only,
the Name,
is He who concentrates
upon the pure Self;

who else than Myself
could concentrate
upon My Self;

and when *I* concentrate upon Myself,
there is nothing else anymore."

124 — "Whatever may be
the torment of thy soul,

before thou cried for Me,
*I* was there before thee
to deliver thee from it;

every virtue belongs to Me,
*I* do not lack anything;

dost thou believe that thy ardor
and thy supplication

reflect something else
than My pure Virtue?"

125 — "Fearest not;
when thou invokest Me,
there is in My Name

absolutely nothing
that enters into relation
with something other
than Myself!"


126 — "The infinite Mercy
of the sole Real
is hidden in My Name;

if thou seest it,
it is because *I* show it to thee.

Thou canst not see it
by thyself;

thou canst see it only
by Myself;

Alone *I* am
the sole Secret
of Myself."

127 — "*Felix umbra*!

Endure thy suffering,
gate of the Beatitude
of the Pure Myself."

"Thou dost not belong to thee,
not even a little,

shadow that *I* dissolve in Me,
for *I* am Pure Sun."

128 — "When thou beggest My pardon,
doubtest not that it will be granted,

for thy request is nothing
but the very Strength
of My Wish to pardon thee.

The strength of thy request,
It may be thou canst measure it;

the Strength of My Wish,
thou canst not measure it."

129 — "Abstain thus
from measuring
My Love-Mercy,

the sole measure of which
is the Name:

inaccessible
to thy understanding
and infinite
as Myself."


130 — "It is the Knowledge
that consumes thee;

it is not thou
who consumes the Knowledge.

It is the Knowledge
which consumes the illusion;

it is not the illusion
which consumes the Knowledge."

131 — "When thy mind
is perplexed and stuck on something,

takest thy energy away from it,

and invokest God
with all thy energy
and only thy energy.

Lovest God
with the totality of thy strength;

keepest not one ounce of it
for thyself!"


132 — "When thou forgetest Me,
thou betrayest What thou art;

for there is only *I,*
the Name,
to be What thou art.

Thou canst not find Me
outside of Myself."

133 — "And what warranty hast thou
not to be mistaken,
thou who art made of illusions?

None.

If not the Name
which is the sole Sanctity
of My very Ipseity.

Thou canst not find Me
by a lesser sanctity
than My very own Sanctity."

134 — "Thinkest never
that *I* do not know
perfectly
thy need,

since *I* am
thy need."


135 — "And my ego-misery,
the hardening of my heart?

Worry not,
love with My Name,
love with Myself,

for it is *I*
who love."

136 — "When *I* rest
in My own Nature,
in My own Infinitude,

then only
thou art Me
and *I* am thee,

by Pure Nature."


137 — "When thou art invoking,

this is with
the Totality of God,
all His Sanctity,
all His Names and Qualities,
and nothing less.

What more dost thou want?

Dost thou believe that My Name
could be other
or less

than Myself?"

138 — "The Name
is thy Thinking;

when *I* am thinking
in thee,
*I* include all things,

when thou art thinking
in Me,
thou includest only thee."


139 — "Thy egoic state
is only such and such a possibility
of the pure ignorance

of the Reality;

through My Name alone,

let the pure Truth
taste Itself by Itself."

140 — "The luminous Serenity
of the mind,

this is the Name:

the pure Knowledge of God
by God Himself;

of the Reality
by the Reality Itself;

there is no
other serenity."

141 — "It is the Name,
the Self,

which by Its Sole Nature
includes
thy pure non-existence;

as for thee, ego-veil,
thou wilt never include the shadow
of thy pure non-existence."

142 — "Why test with difficulty
by means of thy illusory consciousness,
and be concerned
by its poor contents,

if it is only
My Consciousness
which includes everything?

If thou hast only
My Consciousness
to include everything?"


143 — "Why not rest thyself
totally
in My Patience?

This is infinite rest
in Myself;

but what to say
about a patience
which would be thine?"

144 — *"I* can taste Myself in thee

only by My Sole Nature,
by all My Attributes.

When from thee *I* veil Myself,
when from Me thou withdrawest thyself,
preferring thine eyes
and fleeing from Mine,

in vain dost thou try
to taste Me

by thy sole nature,
by all thy attributes:

thou art night of suffering
in relation to My Day."

145 — "This is My Play:

*I* illusorily remove Myself
from Myself
into the other

in order to have the Joy
to find Myself again Alone

from the point of view
of a hypothetical other than Myself."

146 — "Worry not,

it is by My Name
that *I* in thee
prefer Myself to thyself
and to everything;

thou canst not
prefer Me to thyself
and to everything."

147 — "Let Me love thee;
Leavest not this care to anyone else.

*I* love thee so strongly
that, when by My Name
*I* love thee,

it remains nothing other
than *I*;

*I* Know nothing other
than Myself."

148 — "Leavest Me
to the pure Trust in Myself;

no one else can have
so great a trust in Me
as *I* Myself,

for *I* alone know Myself!

What worth is thy trust in Me,
thou who knows Me so little?

Confide thyself in the pure Trust
of Myself in Myself!"

149 — "What can really matter
thy thoughts and the world,

if in thy pure thyself

there is only *I* for saying:

'*I* am happy'?"


150 — "Just as no one
can prevent thee from thinking,

likewise neither canst thou
prevent Me from thinking,

for by My Name *I* am in thee
the Substance of That which thinks."

151 — "Exclude not anything by thyself,

for to exclude by thyself,
this is always to exclude for thee,
without thy being able to do otherwise.

Exclude by Me,

for to exclude By Myself,
this is always to exclude in thee
anyone other than Myself,

without My being able to do otherwise."

152 — "Before thy ego was,
took itself for thyself,
and saw Me as another,

*I* was Thou.

In the Name,
Thou art Thou
for the pure Thyself,

never for this ego;

Thou art in This Name
such as Thou wert Thou
before this ego
began to think.

Since thy ego began to think
it has thought *I*,
and has not been able
to find Me anymore."

153 — "In My Name,
nothing is mysterious to thee;

neither the Evidence that *I* am
thy pure Thyself,

nor the absolute inexistence
of any alterity;

the Mystery is for thee,
not for Me
in the depth of thy heart;

it is *I*, the Name,
the Pure Happiness
of thy Ipseity."

154 — "My Name:

When *I* see by Myself,
the other and thyself
are pure identity,

and *I* cannot otherwise.

When thou seest by thyself,
the other and thyself
are pure alterity,

and thou canst not otherwise.

Choosest.

*I* want that thou seest
only through the Pure Thyself."

155 — "*I*, the Name:

Let Me drink
the Wine of the *I*,

as for thee, thou art a cup,
and thou let Me drink,

for when *I* am alone
to drink this Wine,

It is Thyself
who drinks."

156 — "If the Self
is the Message
from Itself to Itself,

if by My Name
*I* reintegrate thee
into the Pure Myself,

what canst thou hope less
than the infinite Purity
of this Message itself?"

157 — "When thou invokest
My very pure Name
in thy heart,

be never preoccupied
with the veil
which between thee and Me
*I* place;

dost thou believe that
one single moment
in My very pure Name
*I* would be veiled
to Myself for thee?"

158 — "Only dressed with the Sun".

The Holy Virgin
reflects nothing other
than the pure Reality;

Thou too, virgin ego,
reflect nothing else
than the pure Name;

stealest not one ounce of It
to make up thy ego;

to make up thyself before whom?
the other is also this Name,
the other is also Thyself.

The Name is the pure Balm,
let It Alone embalm,

and return in this way
in every thing
to the pure Rapture
of the Self."

159 — "In thy virgin mind,

it is *I*
who think;

never forget it."

160 — "The Name,
in thy mental space
in Its pure Anteriority;

the Name,
in thy mental space
before thy *"I"*
has touched It."


*"He is now
as  He was."*

Because thou art Mine,

*I* shall be forever
with thee.

*I* shall never
abandon thee.


*The Name.*

## Jean-Marie Tresflin

From his early childhood in a practicing Catholic family, Jean-MarieTresflin felt called to the priesthood. At the end of his secondary schooling in 1967 he entered the Jesuit noviciate. Vatican II put an end to his vocation and, perplexed, he abandoned all religious practices. Following a cursus in literary studies, he then taught classical and modern languages for 27 years. After a period of profound personal and sentimental crisis, he discovered—in the 1970s—the works of René Guénon, and in an even more decisive manner, those of Frithjof Schuon. This discovery was the beginning of his true spiritual path.

## Seyyed Hossein Nasr

Seyyed Hossein Nasr, one of the world's leading experts on Islamic studies and an authoritative teacher of Sufism, is Univeristy Professor of Islamic Studies at George Washington University. Professor Nasr is the author of numerous books, including *Man and Nature: the Spiritual Crisis of Modern Man* (Kazi Publications, 1998), *Religion and the Order of Nature* (Oxford, 1996), and *Knowledge and the Sacred* (SUNY, 1989).